SCIFAIKUEST
November 2024

6	A Little Help, Please
10	Editorial
12	The Joshua St. Claire Page
13	The Royal Basinger Page
14	The Stephen C. Curro Page
15	Illustrations by Denise Noe
16	The Denise Hatfield Page
18	The David C. Kopaska-Merkel Page
19	The Gary Davis Page
20	The Ngo Binh Anh Khoa Page
21	The Benjamin Whitney Norris Page
22	The Mark Gilbert Page
23	The Herb Kauderer Page
24	Injecting Fear by Denny Marshall
25	Scifaiku
34	White Snake by Richard E. Schell
	White Snake by Denise Noe
35	Tanka
37	Other Minimalist Forms
51	Article: Etheree by Lauren McBride
52	Article: Gangrene and Gory Ku by Robert E. Porter
57	Featured Poet: D. A. Xiaolin Spires
61	Interview: Tyler McIntosh
65	t.santitoro: my favorite poem

THE STAFF OF SCIFAIKUEST:
TERI SANTITORO, EDITOR

SCIFAIKUEST is published quarterly online and in print. The two editions are different.

Cover art "Space Bride" by Sonali Roy
Cover design by Laura Givens

Vol. XXII, No. 1   November 2024
Scifaikuest [ISSN 1558-9730] is published quarterly on the 1st day of February, May, August, and November in the United States of America by Hiraeth Publishing, P.O. Box 1248, Tularosa, NM 88352. Copyright 2024 by Hiraeth Publishing. All rights revert to authors and artists upon publication. Nothing may be reproduced in whole or in part without written permission from the authors and artists. Any similarity between places and persons mentioned in the fiction or semi-fiction and real places or persons living or dead is coincidental. Writers and artists guidelines are available online at https://www.hiraethsffh.com/scifaikuest.
Guidelines are also available upon request from Hiraeth Publishing, P.O. Box 1248, Tularosa, NM, 88352, if request is accompanied by a SASE #10 envelope with a first-class US stamp. Subscriptions: $28 for one year [4 issues], $44 for two years [8 issues]. Single copies $9.00 postage paid in the United States. Subscriptions to Canada: $33 for one year, $51 for two years. Single copies $11.00 postage paid to Canada. U.S. and Canadian subscribers remit in U.S. funds. All other countries inquire about rates.

What???
No subscription to
Scifaikuest??

We can fix that . . .

https://www.hiraethsffh.com/product-page/scifaikuest-1

Or get a sample back issue to check us out!

https://www.hiraethsffh.com/shop-1

And a subscription makes a great gift, for a holiday or any time of the year!

Minimalism:
A Handbook of Minimalist Genre Poetic Forms

This handbook contains articles about how to write various minimalist poetry forms such as scifaiku, senryu, sijo, haibun, empat perkataan, ghazals, cinquain, cherita, rengays, rengu, octains, tanka, threesomes, and many more. Each article is written by an expert in that particular poetry form.

Teri Santitoro, aka sakyu, who assembled this handbook, has been the editor of Scifaikuest since 2003.

https://www.hiraethsffh.com/product-page/minimalism-a-handbook-of-minimalist-genre-poetic-forms

A Little Help, Please

In the world of the small indie press we fight a never-ending battle for attention to our work, as writers and in publishing. Here's an example: big publishers [you know who they are] have gobs of $$$ that they can devote to advertising and marketing. Here at Hiraeth Publishing, our advertising budget consists of the deposits for whatever soda bottles and aluminum cans we can find alongside the highways. Anti-littering laws make our task even more difficult . . . ☺

That's where YOU come in. YOU are our best promoter. YOU are the one who can tell others about us. Just send 'em to our website, tell them about our store. That's all. Just that.

Of course, we don't mind if you talk us up. We're pretty good, you know. We have some award-winning and award-nominated writers and artists, plus other voices well-deserving to be heard [not everyone wins awards, right?] but our publications are read-worthy nevertheless.

That number once again is:
www.hiraethsffh.com

Friend us on Facebook at Hiraeth Publishing

Follow us on Twitter at @HiraethPublish1

SALE!!

There's a sale going on!!
It's still going on!!

All the books you can order at 20% off the total! Woot!

Buy 1 book; buy 100 books! It's all the same discount. Use the code **BOOKS2024** when you check out.

Go to the Shop at www.hiraethsffh.com and make those selections now!

You'll be glad you did. So will we.

Aliens, Magic, and Monsters
By Lauren McBride

Fun to read. Fun to write. *Aliens, Magic, and Monsters* features poems set in the unlimited and imaginative realm of science fiction, fantasy, and horror. The poems were chosen to showcase over twenty poetic forms from acrostiku to zip, from strict rhyme to free verse, and much more in between. There are guidelines included on how to write each type of poem. Try a sci(na)ku. At only six words, it's sure to interest even the youngest readers.

Type: Juvenile and Young Adult Poetry Manual

Ordering links:
Print: https://www.hiraethsffh.com/product-page/aliens-magic-and-monsters-by-lauren-mcbride

ePub: https://www.hiraethsffh.com/product-page/aliens-magic-and-monsters-by-lauren-mcbride-2

PDF: https://www.hiraethsffh.com/product-page/aliens-magic-and-monsters-by-lauren-mcbride-1

Happy Halloween and Happy Autumn! I hope you enjoyed cavorting in costumes this past Halloween! You're never too old to enjoy dressing-up! Wishing all of our Readers a very Happy Thanksgiving from *Scifaikuest,* and a Merry Christmas, too!

Scifaikuest now has its own ISBN!!! Please inform your local book stores and library that they are now able to ORDER SCIFAIKUEST!!!

You can now find us at Hiraeth Books at:
https://www.hiraethsffh.com/home-1

If you don't have a subscription to our PRINT edition, they are available at:
https://www.hiraethsffh.com/product-page/scifaikuest

And, if you would like to join the select group of contributors by submitting your poetry, artwork or article, you can find our guidelines at: https://www.hiraethsffh.com/scifaikuest

You can also read our ONLINE VERSION at:
https://www.hiraethsffh.com/scifaikuest-online

Pssst! Looking for something good to read?

You can get **t.santitoro's** newest book, *The Red Foil*, a SF mystery, at:
https://www.hiraethsffh.com/product-page/red-foil-by-t-santitoro

You can also get her newest novella, *Those Who Die*, at: THOSE WHO DIE by t. santitoro | Hiraeth Publishing (hiraethsffh.com)

You can also order **t.santitoro's** novella, *Adopted Child*, at: https://www.hiraethsffh.com/product-page/adopted-child-by-t-santitoro

And you can still get a copy of her vampire novelette, *The Legend of Trey Valentine*, at: https://www.hiraethsffh.com/product-page/legend-of-trey-valentine-by-teri-santitoro

Here's a warm Scifaikuest Welcome to our newest contributors: **Mark Gilbert, Tom Guldin, Jazzlyn Huff, Mona Mehas, Jeff Remling, Christopher Sartin, Eddie Spohn,** and **Ryan J.M. Tan**

Thanksgiving feast
a meal of freeze-dried turkey
space station galley

(xeno-unit)

The Joshua St. Claire Page

always
in the last place you look
Higgs boson

cardboard box
without its tape
collapsing star

once again I walk
the sycamore grove...
      but no dryads

struggling to pick out
the androids in the crowd
Barnsley fern

The Royal Basinger Page

gone terraforming
leaving mother earth
nothing but a morning star

gasping for air
in the martian desert
an earthling out of water

finding a place to land
between binary stars
icarus II

The Stephen C. Curro Page

dark matter comet
no one saw
the impact coming

looming kaiju...
its pupil shrinks
to twice my body

Martian sunset
touching the glass
that keeps the air in

twiddling my thumbs...
my AI lawyer argues
with her AI lawyer

Flying Free and Lookie This
by Denise Noe

The Denise Hatfield Page

spring showers
puddle jumping
portals to new dimensions

Wish You Were Here

winter as cold as the grave
tears on a tombstone
fingers wrap around my ankle

waxing crescent
tearing down the moon
using it as a scythe

Dystopia

expanded definition of husbandry
subjugation of women
see also broodmare

Also by Denise Hatfield
Living Bad Dreams

When dreams come alive, there's no telling where they will lead. Everything changes when you realize that, dream or no dream, you're going to die. What do you do then?

Ordering Link:
Print Edition ($9.00):
https://www.hiraethsffh.com/product-page/living-bad-dreams-by-denise-hatfield-1
ePub Edition ($2.99):
https://www.hiraethsffh.com/product-page/living-bad-dreams-by-denise-hatfield-2
PDF Edition ($2.99):
https://www.hiraethsffh.com/product-page/living-bad-dreams-by-denise-hatfield

The David C. Kopaska-Merkel Page

conjoined twins
both hearts given
to the same girl

the ship again
how could I have forgotten
my tether?

Mom and Pop
were the last to go
family meal

the tide returns
another finger
I pluck off your ring

The Gary Davis Page

late Halloween night
weary witches watch TV
Game of Crones

witch flicks switch
snuffs streetlights on Halloween
Jack saves the night

climate-changed Samhain
filthy fingers tote treat bags
melted candy

The Ngo Binh Anh Khoa Page

war museum
all UFO exhibits
serialized and named

fashion runway
new beauty standards set by
new android models

grocery run
the fridge is restocked
with fresh body parts

The Benjamin Whitney Norris Page

ejection

a slippery slope
to the world's edge
spaced by decree

eating for two

eating for two
my hunger
for parasites

stumped

the boy in the sandbox
not biting
all your fingers off

blinding date

a moment of arc
the spark in her eyes
going out with her

my warped drive

my warped drive
parsecs off course
calling for a TOE

The Mark Gilbert Page

threefold symmetry
the alien form
of your genitals

the gyre
of a trash vortex
on Titan

elegantly done
screaming to a climax
and pressing the 'off' switch

The Herb Kauderer Page

time of plenty

food replicator
shaped like cornucopia
all of November

hard choices

bone soup fights hunger
she longs for some company
and misses her dog

Halloween tricks

gifts dropped into bags
an alien invasion
disguised as candy

Injecting Fear
by Denny Marshall

SCIFAIKU

Black Hole

black hole
in the Large Magellanic Cloud:
stargrazing

    James Arthur Anderson

checking the box--
more junk mail
even on Mars

    Albert Schlaht

family reunion ...
the scent of the brimstone
on grandfather's horns

    C. William Hinderliter

UFO crash site
every year around this time
we see the strange lights

    William Landis

smoldering wreckage
from under the white blanket
lifeless tentacle

    William Landis

graves yawn wide
a loved one can't stay
buried forever

    Adele Gardner

a message sent home
light-years crossed in record time
death traveled faster

    Jeff Remling

anger management
won't keep him from seeing red
he's going to Mars

    John H. Dromey

"After the Dance"

finding cinderella next day
leaving behind her foot
reading her metal serial number

    Matthew Wilson

"Broken Lights"

changing overhead bulbs
things in the tank
call them stars.

    Matthew Wilson

armed with your rifle
you paid to be one inch tall
insect safari

    Denny E. Marshall

tears in my eyes
boots on the ground
finally made it to Mars

    Lauren McBride

fusing a new brain
into the tungsten chassis
I smile back at me

    John Hawkhead

quantum paradox
the loss of my particles
as a wave function

    John Hawkhead

across the light-years
particles of dying stars
bombarding the eyes

    E.P. Fisher, PsyD.

a parade
of darkness
lunar eclipse

    Rick Jackofsky

world's food problems solved
growing mushrooms on ourselves
you eat what you are

    Colleen Anderson

new life found
extremophile microbes
in Venus's clouds

    Greg Fewer

cattle rustling
my prize Texas Longhorn
beamed up

    John J. Dunphy

fatal summer
lone corpse swings
watching a Martian sunrise

    Ryan J.M. Tan

spin the crop-circles
messages hidden in wheat
a blueprint revealed

    Wendy Van Camp

Cerberus in Wonderland
caught with the queen's collie
two heads left

    Randall Andrews

practicing safe sex
blindfolded in the bedroom
Medusa's man

    Randall Andrews

dragon mouth casually opens
mammals shriek and flee
dragon breath odor

    Denise Noe

hot buffalo wings
in the colony cafeteria
one wing serves party of twelve

Richard E Schell

med school's first week
anatomy dissection
mom's familiar face

Richard E Schell

dedicates poems
to his koi mistress
mermaid girlfriend

John H. Dromey

Coalescence

tentacles entwined
the acid rain smokes and falls
dissolving our cares away

Eddie Spohn

Reaper's scythe gleams
harvesting souls without pause
your turn

    Yuliia Vereta

death's cold embrace
worldly troubles vanish
peaceful slumber

    Yuliia Vereta

dense fog
blankets the village
onryō seek vengeance

    Christopher Sartin

sharp knife
stabs the silence
sirens scream

    Christopher Sartin

swinging in the breeze
recalling my childhood
the gallows grow dim

    Jeff Remling

old wounds reopened
mad scientist riffles pages
made from human skin

    Guy Belleranti

we peer from shadows
alien lasers wash the buildings
stained glass windows

    Colleen Anderson

Parasitized

Neptunian spring
the egg sac attached to me
starting to twitch

    Eddie Spohn

White Snake by Richard E. Schell

White Snake by Denise Noe

TANKA

searching the wreckage
of my smoking jumpship...
journey's end
the scent of the air
on an alternate world

    C.William Hinderliter

genship romance
the warmth of
my lover's tentacles
pulling me ...
deeper

    C.William Hinderliter

in cramped space warships
crew serve dual roles
chef's warrior skills unsurpassed
his culinary talents not
the greater battle is for takeout

    Richard E. Schell

space bar—
the rhythmic
tapping
of tentacles
on the dance floor

    Rick Jackofsky

legalized cloning–
endless supplies of organs
mass-producing disposable clones
powerless and voiceless
without any legal rights

    Ngo Binh Anh Khoa

ONE-BREATHS
(also Contrails, Tritrails)

amongst Venusian clouds

mating dance of microbes

    Albert Schlaht

OTHER FORMS
(including: Sijo, Fibonacci, Cinquain, Minutes, Diminuendo, Ghazals, Threesomes, Brick, etc.)

RICTAMETER

Dilemma

Humans
All growing wild
(Experiment we lost)
Now moving through the galaxy
Spreading all their species to each star
And sullying our perfect home.
   . . . Their art is grand, it's true . . .
Shall we spare these
Humans?

Doug Gant

Values
Are not as yours
You teach the galaxy
You spread your culture 'cross the stars
But what if we don't want to lose ourselves
What if we don't want these actions
To think the way you do
And adopt your
Values

Doug Gant

ETHEREE

(Here's a form we haven't published in *Scifaikuest* before, with a mini-article below)

After Negotiations Failed

If
the moon
dwellers had
a second chance,
would they attack the
planet below? With so
little gained, so many lives
lost, and the everlasting wrath
of the entire population
of their now estranged, angry ancestors?

Lauren McBride

EPITAPHS

Lazarus The First Vampire

lived twice
died twice
perhaps, third times a charm

Denise Hatfield

Epitaph for a Werewolf

lived and died
by the phases of the moon
playing fetch
with a silver bullet
does not end well on impact

Denise Hatfield

SIJO

galaxies, magnificent energy gems shine in our hopes
each star's core, years of power for Earth's people living cleanly
our vast fleet works light-years' away—
starships arrive to reap Sol

Colleen Anderson

FIBONACCI

she
pulls
the drapes
wide open
morning sun proves it
he's just another faux vampire

David C. Kopaska-Merkel

rare
earth
metals
on the moon
the lunar rebels
want independence
we'll never
let them
have it

T.R. Jones

CINQUAIN

android
almost human
but stronger and faster
threatening to many people
robot

Mona Mehas

JOINED POEMS

SEDOKA

scared to marry
my true love -
a telepath

suppose she asks
if her spacesuit
make her look fat

Lauren McBride

JOINED FIBONACCI

we
don
vampire
costumes and
are pleased at their fake
appearance
because
now
no
one will
suspect our
true identities
until we
expose
our
fangs

Guy Belleranti

when
he
felt a
chill around
the spooky old trunk
he should have
taken
care
but
instead
he raised the
trunk's lid for a peek
and unseen
hands pulled
him
in

Guy Belleranti

RENGA

My Lover

I cannot explain
the rapture of tentacles
I melt under his embrace.

His multiple hands
touch where others cannot reach
life is endless ecstasy.

Mona Mehas

Stray

echoes
before the footsteps
ancestral streets

the year that wasn't
a street with no name

 half a face
the broken mirror
next to my heart

 artifice
learning to play
the local game

 reversed reflection
crossroads as roulette

nonperson
in a strange town
help wanted

aks and dckm

HAIBUN and DRABBUN

HAIBUN

Meanwhile
Tom Guldin

We spiral out of control through the ebony abyss, each passing moment extends our detachment from the known world, the weightless void becomes our constant companion. The starry tapestry, like an uncharted canvas with its secrets veiled in mystery, offers up a myriad of colors enhanced by tracking scopes, as if painted by a cosmic kaleidoscope. Once propelled by purpose and ambition we now simply drift, past veiled gas nebulas no human eyes have seen. Vast, timeless celestial cradles of fledgling stars, still in their infancy, barely glowing.

> our solar collectors
> sit uncharged, unused —
> failed logic of solar drive

Easy Button Reset
Denise Hatfield

Humanity formed the Federation of Earth after years of riots, wars, pollution, and global warming. The F.O.E was tasked with engineering atmospheric control on a global scale. For the first time all minds on Earth came together with one purpose: to save us all and the planet. We terraformed the entire planet into a technological hamster ball and atmospheric crisis was averted. Perpetual comfortable Summers with renewing Spring rain on demand. Earth was thrust into a positive boom in advancement in every aspect. It was not long before the camaraderie dissipated. We cycle, evolve, back pedal to evolve again in all the wrong ways. With time, chaos always worms its way in. Those that could, fled to the new colony on Mars, but most stayed. I pushed the atmospheric airlock control button twenty minutes ago. The sirens blare as the Clash thrashes over the loudspeaker and panicked screams rise as fast as the bodies towards the sky. I hope something worthwhile survives the reset. It is getting hard to breathe.

   shallow breaths
   birth of a new Genesis
   screams lull me to sleep

Thoughts and Prayers
Denise Hatfield

The school's alarm system screeched to life as we sat in Algebra 2. The sounds of shuffling chairs and feet filled the air as we all moved to the back of the room. A maneuver we had practiced many times for a lockdown in case of emergency situations.

"There's been a threat reported next door at Hyde High," Mrs. Thompson said as she went into protocol mode. Her heels clicked on the floor as she locked the door, flicked the lights off and shut all the windows. It grew hot as the soft murmurs around the room died down as we got situated on the floor. A familiar sound from a movie echoed in the room. The racking of a shot gun drew my attention to the person directly behind me. I stared into hollow eyes as an inexplicably painful force slammed into my chest, knocking me the rest of the way to the floor. The ringing in my ears mixed and muffled the cacophony of screaming people as they tried to flee. The reverberating booms and chimes of the shells hitting the floor rocked me to sleep.

    muzzle flash
    high velocity blood splatter
    memorial bouquet of columbines

DRABBUN

Morbid Mile
Denise Hatfield

Traversing the miles on the network of highways is like a worm hole in time. I have an appointment. I arrive just as I'm meant to. Not a minute before or a second later. There's maps and clocks strewn about the cab of my truck. The vehicle changes after every appointment. The clocks and maps never change. Each clock, a token of departure point and time. All roads lead to me. One of the clocks beside me alarms loudly. Mile marker twenty just ahead. The truck lurches and drifts into the median.

   distraction
   high impact collision
   deaths insurance rates soar

***

Country Life Is For The Birds
David C. Kopaska-Merkel

After the mad scientist's stroke the time portal stayed open. A herd of flightless archosaurs consumed the cooling corpse, then escaped through a window of the secluded lab. Farming country, it was, and remnant patches of woodland. Good sources of protein and no large predators. Free-range roosters disemboweled and hens mated, the herd moved on. When the spring chicks hatched they were funny-looking things with voracious appetites. Farmer Smith was missed at the market, but by the time the deputy visited his farm, nothing living remained.

across sunlit fields
we saw them and they saw us
last thought: Jeff Goldblum

Shock To The System
Benjamin Whitney Norris

How I loved her--in the back seat of her father's DeSoto. A warm June day in 1978. Flying saucers in her eyes... Whatever did she see in me?

It wasn't my love that made her do it, in her mother's kitchen. It wasn't my heart she took, that night. All the lights on in the house. Four chambers and no vacancy. Fear of the unknown; the light in the refrigerator that never goes out. It never stops beating, or bleeding.

"Cut it out," I said. "You're scaring me."

> blade gleaming in her hand
> white metal smile
> red lipstick spatters

A Shallow Sanctuary
Randall Andrews

"What's the matter, baby?" asks the outrageously beautiful blonde sitting across from me. "Is the cigar not good?"

With difficulty, I shift my gaze from her to the smoldering Cuban. No, it's perfect. Just like her. Just like the whole stupid place.

"End simulation!" I shout, slamming my fists

against the tabletop, scattering a stack of unpaid bills. My VR implant toggles off, and my tiny, filthy kitchen reappears.

I try to remember the last time I ate. Or showered. Or slept.

Stifling a sob, I whisper, "Resume simulation."

   hurricane of pain
   cyberspace hiding place
   logged in and checked out

Sarrow

Sarrow

The oceans have evaporated as the Earth warmed. It is a time of desolation as the remnants of humanity live in small settlements scattered on what once was the ocean floor. Men are paramount, women are breeders. People do what they can to get by.

One breeder dares to say "No!" to all this: Sarrow. Refusing to breed, and more skilled and resourceful than most men, she sets off to seek her identity and her destiny. Along the way she encounters Karthan, a kindred spirit. Like her, he searches for himself. They are equals.

But the elements conspire against them: earthquakes, salt storms, volcanoes, flash floods. And there are raiding parties who seek to capture and sell slaves. Where are Sarrow and Karthan to go?

Up, says Sarrow. I believe in you, says Karthan. Thus the perilous journey back to the land begins.

https://www.hiraethsffh.com/product-page/sarrow-by-tyree-campbell

ARTICLES

Etheree: A Wedge of Words
Lauren McBride

The Etheree is a relatively new poetic form invented by Etheree Taylor Armstrong (1918-1994), a widely published and highly active poet from Arkansas. The poem is complete at 10 lines starting with one syllable on the first line, and increasing by one syllable on each subsequent line until reaching the final line at 10 syllables. The classic form is a left-justified wedge, unmetered and unrhymed. A title seems to be optional.

As with any poetic form that gains interest, variations arise including being centered, doubled, or reversed.

Anyone familiar with a nonet will notice the similarities between it and a reversed Etheree since they both begin on their longest lines (9 syllables versus 10 syllables respectively) followed by a decrease in syllable count ending in one on the last line. The resultant shape forms an inverted wedge.

In their original forms, the nonet counts down while the Etheree builds up. Even so, the nonet, like the Etheree, can be reversed, doubled, or centered. Conveniently, this lends itself to interchanging the forms for a poem that might require a few more or less syllables to be complete. Perhaps the two forms could be combined into something new.

As the 10 line, 55 syllable Etheree becomes more widely known, it is sure to wedge itself into the ranks of popular minimalist poetic forms.

[For an example, please see the poem, After Negotations Failed, above.]

Gangrene And Gory Ku
Robert E. Porter

"The prosody of haiku," said Kenneth Rexroth, "is totally unknown to almost all haiku devotees in the West and bears exhaustive study, especially by those amateurs who think all you have to do is string together an imagist whimsy in seventeen syllables." (Rexroth)

...And everyone should have translated *100 Poems from the Japanese* into English for New Directions. But we can't all be Kenneth Rexroth.

I had to look up "prosody." It has to do with the Beats of poetry and the rhythm of language. Rexroth was Godfather to the Beats, but he found them – with the exception of Gary Snyder, I think – silly, sloppy, and unsound. So, I'm not sure what he meant by "prosody."

"Almost all translators of haiku," he said, "are pernicious corrupters of taste, as can be studied at leisure in the resulting horrors, the native American 'haiku.'" (Rexroth)

But we look to horror ku *for its horrors*. And to native American ku... for what? The Wendigo? Go Go Gopher teepees flying around like helicopters in early Saturday morning cartoons?

I had to look up "pernicious," too. Big words bother my Little Bear brain. I grew up on Milne and Minarik, with a taste for minimalism. That's my honey-roasted Piglet, my Rabbit fricassee.

More than poor translations annoyed

Rexroth. "The person who thinks he can use D.T. Suzuki or Alan Watts as Baedekers to the actual practice of Japanese Buddhism," he said, "is due for quite a shock when he visits Japan. The theories have as little to do with what happens as the works of St. Thomas Aquinas have to do with the folk religion of the peasants in Aquino." (Rexroth)

Can't that be said of *any* belief system, ever? Statements of belief can be misleading, or misunderstood. Interpretations of scripture change with the hemlines, or the fortunes of war. Religious practices, however, tend to endure; and they can be directly observed. They are the glue that holds a religious community together for generations. As for the duration, I like this ku

> cold Aegean sun—
> the temple
> half stone, half shadow
>   (Forrester)

with its Yin-Yang of stone and shadow, of thing and no-thing. Blank spaces need ink to be legible, or vice-versa. With regard to the Taoist text, Rexroth preferred Arthur Waley's translation. In chapter XI:
> We pierce doors and
>   windows to make
>   a house;
> And it is on these spaces
>   where there is
>   nothing that the
>   usefulness of the
>   house depends.
> Therefore just as we take
>   advantage of what
>   is, we should
>   recognize the
>   usefulness of what

is not._ (Waley, 155)

That's more than a worldview. It's a work ethic.

"The Taoists indeed saw in many arts and crafts the utilization of a power akin to if not identical with that of Tao," said Waley. "The wheelwright, the carpenter, the butcher, the bowman, the swimmer, achieve their skill not by accumulating facts concerning their art, nor by the energetic use either of muscles or outward senses; but through utilizing the fundamental kinship which, underneath apparent distinctions and diversities, unites their own Primal Stuff to the Primal Stuff of the medium in which they work." (Waley, 58)

Hmm...

Ask someone what they *do*, and they'll often tell you what they *are*. I *am* a butcher, for ex., rather than I *butcher* animals. Most stop short of saying they are the meat under their knives, or the door they hang, or the cartwheel, etc. Still, they choose a passive role over the active verb. Why is that? I wonder... If they *are* what they do, how can they do anything else? Put in their place, they put down roots. They take on the mobility of an oak tree or a baobab.

Unlike that woodsman Henry David Thoreau, who compared the Puritan lives and labors of his neighbors to the self-induced suffering of ascetics:

"What I have heard of Brahmins sitting exposed to four fires and looking in the face of the sun; or hanging suspended, with their heads downward, over flames; or looking at the heavens over their shoulders 'until it becomes impossible for them to resume their natural position, while from the twist of the neck nothing but liquids can pass into the stomach;' or dwelling, chained for life, at the foot of a tree; or measuring with their bodies, like caterpillars, the breadth of vast empires; or standing on one leg on the tops of pillars, -- even these forms of conscious penance are hardly more incredible and astonishing than the scenes which I daily witness." (Thoreau, 4)

So, Thoreau went off to live at Walden Pond. He'd show them!

After less than three years, he gave up. Thoreau returned to Concord. "See how he cowers and sneaks, how vaguely all the day he fears, not being immortal nor divine, but the slave and prisoner of his own opinion of himself, a fame won by his own deeds." (Thoreau, 7)

It was worth a try, anyway.

Walden inspired my own determination to keep my costs of living down below the poverty line. As a teenager, I considered buying a friend's pickup truck. The price was right -- until I considered gas, car insurance, maintenance, etc., and converted those dollars into hours of work. I never owned a motor vehicle. I never joined the rat race. I *walk* to a part-time job. I make time for exploring the world around me, for noticing things and talking to people. I'm learning a lot and spending little. So, I can afford to spend many hours researching and writing short essays, like this one, or blackening white pages with gangrene and gory ku.

WORKS CITED

Forrester, Standford M. Untitled. *Haiku in English: The First Hundred Years*. W. W. Norton & Co., 2013. (P. 203.)

Rexroth, Kenneth. "Haiku and Japanese Religion." *The Nation*, 6 May 1968.

Thoreau, Henry David. *Walden and Other Writings of Henry David Thoreau.* Random House, 1950.

Waley, Arthur. *The Way and Its Power.* George Allen & Unwin, 1968.

Postcards From Space
By Terrie Leigh Relf

Here are some messages on postcards from space, found aboard a derelict craft that crashed on an arid, lifeless world. The OSPS (Outer Space Postal Service) has delivered these messages to Terrie, who now presents them to you. This is what it is like out there.

https://www.hiraethsffh.com/product-page/postcards-from-space-by-terrie-leigh-relf

FEATURED POET: D.A. Xiaolin Spires

cool summer nights
fireflies trapped in mason jars
explode in supernova

cigar galaxy
five arms through cut-off sleeves
rev the motorbike's engine

microscopic hairs
wiggle
batting carbon atoms

nonary stars
all lined up
celestial menorah

at the playground
the alien sits alone
tagged "It"

waits for a needle
to be popped
bubble nebula

his saturnian teeth
cavities
the size of her lungs

whirlpool galaxy
add bromine
and soak

milky way
too many biscottis
dipped within

wait a few cycles
the faintest of croaks
tadpole galaxy

cigar galaxy
wrapped in leaves
billowing silvery smoke

nuclear
fusion-fired
best pizza in the universe

drunken hiccup
from their lips
a civilization is born

the hive mind collapses
thirty thousand beings
one will and testament

(optional title: *at the space station*)

illegally parked
space shuttles
sport matching boots

(optional title: *u-pick at the exoplanet*)

juicy plums
nestled within
their cold plumage

(optional title: *fooled by the gps*)

a left onto milky way
spiraling down all its arms—
never arriving at candy land

sinkhole
my prefrontal
caves

shouting match
the flicker
of stars

silky strands
ramen rays slurped up by
telescopic eyes

INTERVIEW WITH FEATURED POET D.A. Xiaolin Spires

How long have you been writing poetry?

I may have written poems prior to this, but the first I recall is writing for a school assignment and I accompanied the poetry with an illustration. Thematically, I recall it had to do with the moon and its ethereal beauty. It's stuck in a hard drive in a defunct computer somewhere, I'm sure... and perhaps its printed form is turning brown, oxidizing somewhere in a box.

Do you write poetry other than genre poetry? If so, what kind?

Much of my poetry is speculative in some form or other, but I do write poetry about mundane life or the universe around me, sometimes sardonic and sometimes simply in appreciation or awe. I also write speculative short stories, from microfiction to novelettes to longer works.

Who is your favorite poet?

I'm not sure I have a favorite, but I have some fond memories of reading and dissecting e e cummings, William Carlos Williams, Robert Frost, Gwendolyn Brooks, Bashō, Federico Garcia Lorca and the like growing up and through adulthood. I really enjoy immersing in the poetry of some of my contemporaries and fellow contributors, in speculative fiction/poetry magazines and chapbooks, in English and in other languages. Some of these poems make me exasperated, some make me laugh, some make me go "hmmm" that's interesting! Some are awe-inducing. Some make me hungry, grossed-out or inspire the senses in other ways. Some have cool shapes and forms. As for examples of poems in other languages, some works that come to mind are the speculative poetry of Ko Hua Chen and the poems in this recommendation of Japanese scifaiku (with English translations) by Taku Nakajo in the magazine Anima Solaris. http://www.sf-fantasy.com/magazine/column/scifaiku/20030401.shtml

What/who is your main inspiration?

Science, technology, ecology, food, everyday life, our absurd and lovely human cultures, travels for research, prompts from my writing group and my anthropological background.

Whose poetry has influenced you the most?

n/a (Same answer as "Who is your favorite poet?")

Did you begin writing haiku before you branched out to scifaiku?

n/a (I can't recall)

How did you learn about scifaiku?

n/a (I'm not sure... I think from magazines? Or maybe from my writing group? Or maybe much earlier?)

What poetry magazines do you read/contribute to?

Besides Scifaikuest, *I enjoy the works of and contribute to* Star*Line, Eye to the Telescope, Dreams and Nightmares, *and speculative fiction magazines that also publish poetry such as* Uncanny, Analog, Lady Churchill's Rosebud Wristlet, Lontar, Liquid Imagination, Polu Texni, Mithila Review, Grievous Angel, Silver Blade (some of which are unfortunately no longer publishing new issues). *I also recommend the podcast of Deborah Davitt,* Shining Moon, *with improv speculative poetry appearing in specific episodes.*

What micropoetry forms would you like to write more in:

haiga (yes to illustrations!)

chained cinquains

more scifaiku!

D.A. Xiaolin Spires steps into portals and reappears in sites such as NY, Hawai'i, various parts of Asia and elsewhere, with her keyboard appendage attached. She has a Ph.D. in socio-cultural anthropology, writes speculative fiction and poetry, teaches martial arts, paints fantastical art in sumi ink and acrylic and convenes around tabletop games and RPG's. Her multifaceted writing, including fiction and non-fiction, reflects her interest in food systems, ecology, technology and society. Her stories appear in *Clarkesworld, Uncanny, Nature* and *Galaxy's Edge*—and have been selected for The Year's Top Robot and AI Stories and The Year's Top Tales of Space and Time Stories. Her poetry has been nominated for the *Dwarf Star, Rhysling, Best of the Net* and *Pushcart Awards*.

FAVORITE POEM

hard choices
Herb Kauderer

bone soup fights hunger
she longs for some company
and misses her dog

WOW! If ever a scifaiku told a complete and poignant story, it's this one! This is absolutely AWESOME, Herb! Well done! Thank you!!
--t.santitoro, editor

www.ingramcontent.com/pod-product-compliance
Lightning Source LLC
LaVergne TN
LVHW012036060526
838201LV00061B/4642